THE EDGE OF THE SCREEN

The EDGE OF

JOEL LANE

THE SCREEN

PUBLICATIONS
1999

Published by Arc Publications
Nanholme Mill, Shaw Wood Road
Todmorden, Lancs. OL14 6DA

Copyright © Joel Lane 1999

Design by Tony Ward
Printed at the Arc & Throstle Press
Nanholme Mill, Todmorden, Lancs.

ISBN 1 900072 14 9

ACKNOWLEDGEMENTS
Thanks are due to the editors of the following
magazines and anthologies: *Ambit; Blade; Dog;
The Echo Room; Envoi; Foolscap; The Gregory
Anthology 1991-1993; Headlock; Jugular
Defences; The New Statesman & Society; The
North; Other Poetry; Outposts; Oxford Poetry;
People to People; The Printer's Devil; Private
Cities; The Rialto; Scratch; Spokes; Sunk Island
Review; Tandem; Tears In the Fence; The Third
Alternative; Verse; The Wide Skirt.*

The author gratefully acknowledges the financial
assistance of the Society of Authors.

Thanks are due to the following for help, support
and encouragement:
Steve Anthony, Veronica Bradney, the Cannon Hill
Writers' Group, the Cannon Poets, Peter Coleborn,
Robert Cooksey, Sarah Crowther, Dad, Peter
Daniels, Paul Drohan, Carol Ann Duffy, John
Harvey, Dorothy Hunt, Richard Jones, Graham
Joyce, Helen Kitson, Rupert Loydell, Simon
MacCulloch, Ian McMillan, Chris and Pauline
Morgan, David Morley, Clare Morrall, Mum,
Joseph O'Neill, Greg Oxnard, Mike Parker, Kate
Pearce, Jeff Phelps, Neil Powell, Deryn Rees-Jones,
Mark Robinson, Nick Royle, Gina Standring, Elly
Tams, Tony Valentini, Virtue Without Terror, Tony
Ward, John Wells, Conrad Williams, Jane Wright,
Peter Wyles.

The publishers acknowledge financial assistance
from Yorkshire & Humberside Arts Board.

CONTENTS

For Paul Drohan –
the fighter still remains

I
TERRITORIES

INVERTED TREES

I visited her in hospital again today.
She was sleeping. On the way home,
I saw children wearing those masks.
Only the poor ones show their faces
on city streets. The autumn light
sticks to you like clingfilm.

At night, the buildings shake
from passing lorries. Is it true
they're carrying tanks of nitrogen,
oxygen, the elements of clean air?
For private use. Sometimes I dream
of a block of air, gently smoking.

After a thunderstorm, a faint smell
of vomit hangs in this district.
Rotten brick. I go to the ward
nearly every day. She can't speak
any more. I remember the forest
where we used to walk together,

the trees reflected in the still lake.
Her lung X-ray. How on our first
night together, she gave me air.
Her mouth sealed on mine, ribs
letting go. I can still taste it –
burning, anaerobic, but not stale.

Behind a barred window and a padlocked door
he'd made a private chamber of echoes.
From the radio station, painted like a schoolroom
in green, he broadcast old records and chatter
to the staff and patients of an asylum.

It gave him a place to be himself,
somewhere to bring his friends, to be heard
and not seen. It gave him voices
for all the aching moments: shelved
in the raw archive of past songs.

He could call on a thousand dry throats,
hearts worn on numbered cardboard sleeves,
dry eyes and dusty stumbling tracks
and Dusty Springfield – the old traumas
that he mimed as the records played.

Between tracks, he'd always ask
the listeners to phone the station's number
with their dedications or requests.
Nobody ever rang. Off microphone
he swore at his mute audience:

"Talk to me, you bastards!"
His face changed from mock anger
to real unease, as much lost then
as he was at home. I thought
of de la Mare's "one man left awake".

He locked up the station in darkness,
and we passed through the stone arch
and the hospital grounds, held back
from the road by high spiked railings.
We waited, feeling cold, in a bus shelter

whose glass was splintered on the pavement.
Across the main road, some black houses
stood behind an acre of waste ground;
at our backs, the Victorian hospital buildings
kept their people shut up and shut off.

SAVING FACE

Scar city is the brief: the null slogan
that underwrites the ad men
who've put up huge billboards
by the side of the expressway,
screening off the derelict houses
and patches of wasteground from view.

Near the industrial district, half
a street's worth of wire fence
surrounds a building site: trenches
and wooden crosses in the mud.
The contractor's logo on a red sign
declares the enterprise: MEND-A-CITY.

THE TOWER

Last night, the couple next door were beaten
by youths wearing gloves. They sprayed
red letters in the stairwell: AIDS CARRIERS
LIVE HERE. Is the tower of the *Daily Star*
as tall as this? Do those quotes echo

between its floors? *I'm afraid of touching
the lift doors, in case of infection.*
(Published without comment.) You want to say:
rest easy, nothing can harm you. Eyes
that never open are safe from blindness.

Meningitis can't touch a concrete skull. But
this morning, the walls are bruised with cold.
Yes, people have died here. Friends of yours,
not things from the pit. The lift reminds you
of how, eight years ago, you went up

like a nerve impulse in a spinal column
until its shivering box discharged you
to the cell of a lover's flat, his arms.
They are building a tower of ignorance
to trap you, and everything you know, inside.

*We wear gloves to operate the lift. We're
terrified.* Fear builds on fear. You walk
up twelve flights of stairs, to see the dawn
above the city. But the view's overgrown
with towers; no window is high enough.

NEAR GOLD

By the time we found the house,
the sun was a small coin, near gold,
at eye level; it threw our shadows
across the doorstep, ahead of us.
The rooms had filled up with night;

we stumbled past the veiled mirror,
the crippled staircase. The back door
was already open; the path lost itself
in a field of wheat and silver grass
dissolving in seeds. Rain had broken

the back of a premature harvest.
A few unbound sheafs, near gold,
waited for the landowner's van.
You pulled me down to the stubble,
and kissed me as though trying

to draw the breath from my lungs.
"Tell me what's gone wrong here
in our field, there in our house.
Explain it." I pressed your face
against my chest, out of sight.

But your eyes, sharpened by tears,
stared into me. Their darkness
was the answer: something like rain,
a foreclosure of open spaces.
Fear. I pushed it away

and held you at arm's length.
"Listen to me. You're the one
who couldn't wait for anything.
You had no time for husbandry.
This is your here and now, love:

14

harvest home. This rotting field
at the back of a derelict house.
You forced years into a season,
feeding your eyes, not the soil.
Don't blame me." You shut up

for good, then. Your grim face
was pale as a stillborn baby's.
You helped me soak the dark field
in petrol, and set it alight,
throwing on books, letters, photos.

We sheltered in the empty house,
watched the fire from an upstairs window
and made love on the dusty floor.
Traffic passed on the other side,
worrying at the city's throat.

The next time I saw you
you'd bleached your hair, near gold.
You'd moved in with a new lover,
and you sat blowing dandelion clocks
over his living-room carpet.

THE LIVING CARPET

We were a small company, in a building
so old we shared office space with ghosts.
And other things, as we found out

that first imprisoned winter. Eight people
off sick at once wasn't just bad luck.
Black lumps in the kitchen weren't coffee grains.

Rentokil told us the whole structure
was riddled with gaps like Emmenthal:
between floors, behind walls. And then

the itchy ankles. Skin burning like paint.
That thick, white carpet we'd all admired
was full of mites. *We need to damp down*

this mass hysteria, the manager said.
Our eyes focused on microscope slides:
faecal pellets, tiny arthropods, the white

atmosphere of the clinic. After work,
three of us escaped to the nearest pub
and sat talking for hours, feeling alcohol

tighten in our throats and blood vessels,
watching our fears crawl. The two
youngsters, fresh from college, kept on

touching each other's arms – not quite
ready to kiss in public, but needing
something bigger than themselves to hold onto.

THE SECOND FLOOR

These old houses. It's strange
to live in a flat that was once
just a room. There are echoes
in the stairwell, the ghosts of children.
These rooms on the second floor
were all bedrooms once. Now
they're partitioned, locked up.

At night, I see double beds
being pushed along the roadway,
like some fund-raising event.
And I wake up cold, knowing
that the second floor is the street.
I've known it all my life,
but I still can't get used to it.

PASSIVE VOICE

She's made up her mind to leave him,
though he's not ready. Neglect
has locked her out of her own rooms.
So many things to be done,
and all the dues unpaid, the damage
unmended, adds up to a guilt
like a second mortgage on the same house.

She's thrown so many coins down into
this whitewashed stairwell, and none of them
even caught the light in falling.
Escher might have sketched in her lover
there, stepping over her gifts; always
climbing hard, but ending up further down.

She wakes him on Sunday morning
with a drink of water; the glass
is cracked, but the water is clear.
Daylight hardens his tender cheeks
with the blind ash of generations.
He cuts the stubble, drowns it, comes
back to bed a tired smiling boy.
It's her life that the beard clings to,
his needs ingrained in her; they itch,
but she can only scratch the windows.

Only she really lives here. He moves
on a staircase, grounded with each step:
a laugh, a caress, a promise, a meal.
She's made up her mind to leave him,
though she wants to remake him for herself
the way she built a face, long before,
with torn paper and glue on a wire skull.
She wants to hold the pain he ignores.

The mesh of summer, dry-eyed and porous,
sifts the day. Above and below them
the other tenants are waking up.
Music fills the house, one room at a time.
She knows them all, single and paired;
they come to her for cigarettes or help.
She hoards their names, her unclear family.

Last night, she dreamed of the basement
with its faint neon tube, its plaster walls
where damp had shaded in a forest.
All the tenants were there, gathered
around her where she lay crooked
on the cement floor, her mouth widening
like oil on water; until the ghost
reached from her throat with a clean hand.

OPEN SECRET

You'll never mention that you were here.
Whatever you see, there are no witnesses.
You are only an audience. The fires
are burning, but they make no sound.

These are the crimes of the decent
against the tainted. No evidence
can get through the wires. These men
are so young, their stubble washes off

in the petrol-tinged rain. Women
cry out, but it's not on record.
Too late. You grip the chain-link fence
and start to weep; your own silence

rings in your ears. Whichever side
you're on, the fence is still there.
Walk now. Distance forgets. It's cold
enough; leave these images behind.

Let the stain under the closed body
be its shadow. At the perimeter
of the circle, people are standing
to look out or look in. No-one speaks.

It leaves me cold. This morning
I walked through Digbeth, its oppressive
Victorian buildings draining colour from
the world; in the coach station
I saw a woman nursing a bottle wrapped
in a shawl. If I had a camera
that image is what I would have sent you.

Above the fairground, the empty wheel
turns like a projector after the film
has run out. Once I seemed to fall
for your mimicry of experience, the damaged
youth in your eyes. It's just a stage
you're going through, via the trapdoor.
You've turned the city into a village.

I can't do this any more. I'd never
have guessed how trying to be young
can drain you. This is the close season;
maybe I'll be back. The fairground will stay
with me, inside – however rusty, however
unsafe. We stay the same: preferring
fucks to friendship, fireworks to the sun.

He told me how he had taken the last
train to the coast, to watch the tide
go out; he walked miles over the unlit sand,
until his feet were numb, then found a hotel.
"My God, it was cold." Still, the sea had taken
the harpoon of his fear, and broken it free.
As he spoke, the brick of houses dissolved;
the wind blew inside their frames,
carrying grains of light to his face.

Nothing breaks the gravel skin
of the school playground where children scatter,
crested with urgency. I watch them
through the railings. This tide shrugged
me off, once, still breathing to its pulse,
still with salt in my mouth. From that wall
a girl of eight borrowed a carved face
to tell me: if you don't follow God
you are following the Devil. Now the voices
break in air, almost coherent, like sleet
just before it reaches the window.

Once the walls have been restored,
the scaffolding is removed; those who live
in these buildings cannot see their frames.
No-one would think the grey cliffs formed
from the spittle of tides; unless perhaps
they saw the fossils that defaced them,
the fingernails and teeth that we left
embedded, our hostages, in walls
that were more real than we expected.

II
ICONS

FOR WINGED ANTS

The 'Mr. Whippy' type of soft ice-cream was developed by a team of food technologists which included Margaret Thatcher.

Team nothing: it was her creation.
In years to come, it would be judged
her greatest achievement. Generations
would swear by its clinical taste, its odd
coolness. (She'd never been keen on milk.)

Now, released from the chains of solidity
and freshness, it could be sold anywhere
by anyone, and still be the same.
Air was the key: a crafty foaming,
like rubber or polystyrene, between the spout

and the cone. Air gave grace and form
to non-milk fat and sugar; the power
to inflame a thirst while pretending
to quench it. A half-melted candle
for winged ants to fight over, like

those viscous white coils deposited
by certain well-bred dogs. Its lack
of authenticity was a mark of pride,
a sheen. Everyone wanted to lick it.
In blue light, it could become a torch.

REHEARSAL

It was an ordinary night. After a gig.
First thing I knew, his glass smashed
on the floor. Like a sound-effect.
When I saw his face tighten,
a riff started playing in my head.

It was another fit. Or the hospital drugs.
Or some desperate madness; I don't think
anyone could have said by then.
I remember him hitting the wall, clawing.
We didn't stop him. Paint. Wallpaper.

Plaster. Brick. And he was still
climbing the steps of our music,
just like on stage. He turned round,
his fingers webbed with blood.
Now it was our voices trying to pull

him out. But he'd pushed his head
through some barrier, some alley into
nothing. I remember the darkness
tearing his mouth apart. I saw it,
heard it, all through what came after.

On dry land she was clumsy.
The wind pulled at her hair.

But she was a fine swimmer:
powerful lungs, a strong heart;

her voice was like a man
and a woman arguing it out.

She always swam underwater,
freed by pressure on all sides –

away from the weight of things, from air;
floating and sinking at once.

With vodka burning in her guts
and her mouth taut with nembutal,

she tried to draw a breath
at the wrong moment.

What came to the surface was swollen
with fame, but it wasn't her.

It was Michelangelo who spoke
of looking for the body in stone,
hidden from eye or hand. That night
you read the words, and couldn't sleep
for the chafing of discovered limbs;

the next morning, clear in mind,
you waited outside the museum
with a sack of cold granite chips
and glue and Government authorisation
to reconstruct the featureless block.

COLD AS STONE

Long after the last of the Saturday night drinkers
had staggered home, she left the house
where Carl was sleeping on the couch downstairs.
They'd been up half the night, and broken
every plate made by the craft of their love:

bone china, glaze-effect, willow pattern,
geraniums. He'd said, whatever they felt
or didn't feel, whatever was wrong between them,
the sacrament still counted. To lose that
was to break light into chunks of darkness.

I don't believe you, she thought. Now
she was outside the church, with no coat
between her and the February night. *Shit
this*. She knew she'd never come here again.
Then she was kneeling among the graves –

not to pray, she was crying too hard
to stand. At the back of the church,
a streetlamp touched a wall of grey stones
through the bars of a poplar. *No more*.
Each of the stones was a window

on a tiny cell, where a baby was kept
in stillness. As the wind reached them
they all began to shiver and cry out;
hardly alive. She couldn't tell who
would die from exposure and who would grow.

Neither of them knew. She went home,
packed a bag, caught a train to her sister's
through the midnight of Sunday morning.
She thought of Carl; looking at a bare field
through mist, she saw him waking up.

SKID MARX

That mystery skin; those bloodshot eyes.
He's talking fast, hard, dangerous,
the mic halfway down his throat.
Every gesture sneers, face upward.
The pain is sharp. The pain is real,

too deep for stitching. The cropped hair.
He's a scar. An icon for a culture
where violence has no script.
A killer's eyes in a victim's face
(or was it the other way round?)

Skid was born on the front page.
The year's most radical newcomer:
pure anger, pure hate. He must have
been through Hell to feel that way.
His sex is a political energy

and his politics are totally erotic.
Those who can't stomach his
radical jive, his knife in the mind,
evidently have no balls. He's
always quoted out of context,

always. If he spat at outsiders,
if he wished the innocent dead,
it was for a good reason: to shock
all the *middle class liberals*
who everyone hates, worse than Hitler.

Mornings in the jacuzzi, his colour
washes out. Not mixed-race at all
but dead white. As white as leukaemia.
He stripped the blood from others;
dying already, they didn't mind.

COLLABORATION

He's hanging in the doorway again,
blowing kisses at me from the canal's
oily mirror. He's lying in my bath,
arms sleeved with blood, a red hem
spreading over his knees like a dress.

How can I be where he is: a world
infected with his stillness? He knows
I want to go there, make him real.
It's not on. How could he answer
the phone, be there on time, smile

when it was needed? Meanwhile,
I wake up with him. For comfort
I wear him under my skin. Let him
face the cracked February daylight.
He reads the paper, signs forms,

handles money. Nobody catches on.
He combs finely through the motions.
Shrink-wrapped around his cool head,
I feel open to the world. Stroke me
and I'll give you my heart, my vote.

THE HIGH NOTES

It's on the tape of songs you gave me.
Her voice fleshing out the piano keys;
an eye without a map, free to rework
the fabric of sunlight. Pure notes
for an impure life; unbroken vowels
tinged red by the breaking of veins.

Your love life is like your faith,
warm reality built on abstractions.
All your certainty is in the walls.
Inside, the room is cold; voices
turn white, clouds become statues
with echoes for wings. Outside,

the walls are cracked and grimy
from passing traffic. People are still
touching the stones, wondering what
they did wrong. You're out here too –
one of us, shivering in a trenchcoat
with its pockets full of cassettes.

MIMESIS

What he was trying to prove
I don't know. Three or four years
older than me, he capered
and sneered and flapped his hands
and followed me home from school,
spitting on the back of my coat.

In bad light, I stare at the mirror;
criticise my stance, gestures, script.
Behind me he is dancing; half
my age now, but still older. My disgust
against his. It makes no sense.

I know the cost of dry cleaning
is beyond me; but I don't know
how much blood I have to spill,
or which of us will give up first.

HARD TO FIND

Sound is a bastard to work with.
It's too human. The severed chords
fall in the image of believers, those
defined by their needs. An audience,
an obsessive lover, the blind unborn.

It's not a style. Muttered words,
violent guitars; you only raise
your voice when screaming. Now
you've pieced together the mirror,
but the image is still broken.

Mind. The white noise of pain
reduces you to an echo, your trace
preserved in the mix. The last sound
you hear is not a human voice.
They'll suck the hole in your head

to feed their loss. A child cries.
Nothing is transformed. All this week,
the rain tastes bitter and the sky
itches, trying to close itself up.
Your silence will go platinum.

COLD WAR TACTICS

It began with sharing: *us and them.*
Late nights at the pub's barricade
that left his clothes encoded with smoke.
Bus-stop skirmishes never made contact
with the real enemy. He had to get
to know it through a life of espionage.
His companions became strangers.
He never came in from the cold:
grim, compromised, he fought on alone.

There were contacts. Nocturnal visits
to his flat, made by enigmatic women
with fur hats between their legs
and breasts as pale as the frost
on a bottle stored in a deep freeze.
Red label, blue label, black label –
he learned the difference, then forgot it.
Sometimes he'd wake up alone
in the bare ruins outside the wall,

staring at deformed faces, reaching
with hands that turned to stone,
shivering. When the wall fell down
he kept one chunk of broken glass
as a newly opaque souvenir.
Clutching his side, he wiped the light
from the mirror. Saw his own mock-heroic
pose, the lines of a fake war, and its truth:
poverty, four decades of waste.

MICHEL FOUCAULT

Your illness was bad enough. The frantic
rush to finish that last book
when the work could never be finished.
All your life, you'd wanted to be a chisel

and not a statue. You'd struck history
at an angle, exposing the fault lines;
always leaning, because the world
was tilted. Pleasure came late,

peace never at all. You were locked back
in your first prison, 'the black stone
of the body' – passive, inscribed
with the stigmata of someone else's

knowledge. The chisels of loss
took your resistance – then chipped away
the shells, one skin at a time. Prayer
and sweat, a damaged being; the things

you went to California to escape.
Full circle. Just as you'd written it:
how the human clay was mass-formed
in factories, schools, prisons, hospitals;

in the confession box, on the couch.
Did you guess how you'd be reborn
as an Icarus on the point of falling –
a postmodern icon, made up of dots

on a screen, revelations on a glossy page?
All the private details: the handcuffs,
the molten wax? Hacks consigned you
to the prison of the flashbulb. A fuck

doesn't merit death or facile celebrity.
But you always knew. There's no place
called freedom. Only these words, these
movements; a level exchange of glances.

THE EDGE OF THE SCREEN

The night has a thousand cameras.
But the film of sweat between his hands
is drying already
as his body folds across itself
like a discarded bit of celluloid

in the streetlamp's pool of light
outside the nightclub
where his friends have just stopped playing.
A hidden box of paints
has coloured his mind. The autopsy

will reveal a cracked bandage,
the flakes of limestone scale, whatever.
The poisons have nowhere to run to.
A thin hospital fluid develops
the night's exposures:

another shadow peeled off
from the industry of vision.
Another carbon tracing
of one body, its painful energy
printed onto a concrete slab

here at the road's edge
where sirens call to each other.
There is too much empty space
they have to get through,
and their destinations are too quiet.

MAGAZINES

Where did they all get to?
There were four of us in that house.
One's living in Appendix, Ohio,
faxing articles to gay magazines.

Another's got back together
with his wife; last I heard
he'd sold photos of her
in a leather catsuit. Kitsch,

not porn. A film magazine.
He told me about the third:
seven staircases down
in Hotel Paranoia, living

on Snickers bars and Coke,
obese now, sleeping rough
in the computer department
at the University, surfing

the Internet all night.
"You can't get through to him."
Me, I live with my job,
but we argue like old drunks.

It can't go on like this.
In the dark, I turn over
the pages. A fringe, a smile,
an open hand. Last week

I drank a jar of dried flowers
and wrote on a birthday card,
stay young. We're all in love
with the evidence, the hard copy.

This used to be a playground;
now it's an art gallery.
I think of cyberspace: pageless
text, infinity, madness.

III
MESSAGES

MESSAGES

A friend, passing the hostel one night, threw
gravel at my window to summon me.
Now rain makes the noise of tearing sheets
against the glass; or of trapped wings.
Something wants to escape or break in.

Last week, the gale that made headlines
slammed back an open window and smashed it.
A language student wrote these words,
neatly, in pencil on the kitchen wall:
Mon Dieu, aide moi. Je t'en supplie.

Some drunk on the third floor ran
back and forth in the night, punching
doorframes, shouting *Does he fuck? Does
he fuck?* The fracture of privacy
creates isolation; so do the thefts,

and the rules barring overnight visitors.
It's mid-February; a lack of messages
can hurt. Even when the clouds lift
the light is dispersed, without a focus.
A winged foot has sprained its ankle.

CUT

Still bright, the trail of his blood
froze the roadway. A single frame:
one still on the cutting-room floor.
He was lying between a shop window
and a streetlamp, his eyes closed.

The manager of the bar called
his name, held him. She sent me
back inside to fetch tissues and ice.
(I found the ice.) The doorman
claimed he'd found him like this.
She stared at his hand, the rings.

The boy's face was a jigsaw drawn
in blood; she knelt and wiped it clean.
One gash, like a tilted eyebrow,
caught the yellow light, killed it.

GLASS HOUSES

The needle stalled; a moment's
silence became a new track.
We called to find each other,
stared with our hands.

Outside, it seemed worse;
car drivers were projectionists,
the skyline was missing.
After half an hour, someone

knocked. A young woman:
"Candles for sale. Fifty pence each."
You laughed, said it was
enterprise culture. I paid.

On the main road, other
people were making a profit.
Twelve shops looted. The streets
were paved with glass.

No bloodshed; no riot.
They drove in, took
what they wanted and left.
A helicopter circled

to freeze-frame the road
with its white gaze. When
the lights came back on,
the room stank of wax.

So did the newspapers,
printing fire. When the dark
unites us, we shed images.
(Forty televisions were stolen.)

BACKTALK

Coming into Oldbury, the bus passes through
an abandoned council estate: three or four
layers of cubes, featureless, broken;
like something in a nursery school. But
people lived there, perhaps still do. The station
is a gallery of black numbers. On a wall

someone has written HAVE A GOOD FUCK
IN HELL YOU STUPID BASTARD. Someone
got stood up. It feels less than real:
the giant layers of car parking space
around the drive-in McDonald's; the one
hypermarket instead of a shopping centre.

I wonder if it's just me. My lack
of sleep. Near the Health Centre, three men
are sitting on a bench, smoking. I walk
towards them, my mouth hanging open
like an idiot's. And pass them.
It makes me realise just how much

reality is in the head, or in words.
When he said *I can't stand it here
on my own, I need someone with me
to talk to,* I thought he was weak.
Depressed. But now I can see it;
I only have to think *this is my home*

and the light cuts like paper. Friendship
can leave you open. Insomnia is catching.
Lost already, I check the A-Z map.
*Why the road signs? These aren't roads.
They go nowhere. No pavements. No houses.
Language doesn't belong here.* Shut up.

Past an industrial estate, another, then
another. Then a few tower blocks
clustered on some uneven wasteground.
Children stone an old van. *Don't let
this be where my friend lives.* It is.
He's in; that's good. His brother

is there too; that's better still. But
after half an hour of sitting in his flat,
the walls seem about to cave in.
Sean never opens the curtain; I glimpse
the view and understand why. He
points to the doorframe. "Last week

I nearly decided to break the glass
up there, hang myself in the doorway.
I'm not joking." His brother says,
"You don't have to tell me. I know
what you'm like." We smile. The light shifts.
We drink Lilt, make plans for the evening.

TELL ME SOMETHING

Why I'm trying to give you a strength
I don't have. The air strings
beads on the rim of your glass,
soaking your hand. Why the sleet

looks so alive in flight, when
it tastes as blank as this.
Your smile's a crystal of pain,
your face is a paper lantern

with shadows trapped under it.
Why tomorrow, you'll go to see a man
when the stitches are still in your head
from the last time you met him.

NIGHT VISION

She called him her little fox
for his spiky hair, his small nose
and his ability to see in the dark.
She made a lair for him, used
words like *hibernate* and *forage*

and loved him through the winter.
In the spring, she found someone else:
a man who played bridge to win,
who was bearded, ambitious, not so cute.
He took to walking around at night

while she was out. Once he saw
a dead fox lying beside the wire fence
on the edge of the park. It smelt cold.
Not so cute, to have insects crawling
on your face. To feel the way he feels now.

DEFROSTING

This meat has been
too long in the freezer:
it's bruised with ice.
Thawed, it will stink.

The pale walls upstairs
ache; I can't feel it.
Time shines. But soon
you'll warm me to pain.

You said you'd just
give him a lift home.
The timer on the fridge
counts minutes, then hours.

You phone; your voice is
soft with apology.
I wonder: is the bed
half empty or half full?

REAL TIME

That weekend, they were a couple: driving
a hundred miles of motorway and urban sprawl
to an historic town, and a hotel bedroom.
The crystal of time hardened in their mouths.

Sunlight danced on the windscreen, the window;
under the steady and bright microscope
of desire, the patterns grew. Completeness
was near enough to struggle for.

They both had lovers waiting at home –
the one in New York, knowing nothing;
the other not far away, knowing enough.
You phoned me twice from the hotel.

The pattern's still growing, discreet
as a computer virus; there's no screen.
We all live in the same time. Whatever
we use up, someone else has given.

The house is quiet now. Our throats
are dry from each other's words.
I'm draining sour gold from a bottle
as you drive off into a storm of light.

A PRO FORMA VALENTINE

The couple struggling in my dream
are linked by the darkness within them –
legs spread like antennae, shoulders
rippling with surface tension. No
archetype floats behind them: only
a pale-faced boy with dead eyes
whose world is Harp cans and enemies,
and a sneering girl in a black skirt
stubbing a cigarette out on her own hand.

And behind them, only the narrow faces
staring like holes from upper windows.

I don't know what to write to you,
[insert name], hunting for work and friends
in this city of façades and building sites
and vomit stains and telephone boxes.
I can't make this place your home, only
do God knows what damage by trying.

THE ONLY LANGUAGE

You've half an hour between trains.
Long enough for a coffee, a newspaper,
a cigarette; but not long enough
for a meal, a drink, or a decent cry.
Long enough to make a phone call.

It's late evening. The station concourse
fills up with vagrants, stretched
out on benches. A young woman
looks straight at you, and you realise
she's a man. You want to stop,

but the train's moving in your head.
Outside is a white jigsaw. Your eyes
are cold; it must be the wind.
A telephone box. You remember
the area code. Ring, ring, click:

the edge of his recorded voice
scrapes your memory. You wait until
the tone, then speak. *It's me.*
I'm coming back. I promise. He'll know
exactly what you mean by that.

ENGAGED

You're talking slate. Chalk couldn't mark
its tacky slope. You're talking hailstones
spattered against all the small panes
on the outside of this telephone box.

You're talking spider's web, too thin
to catch anything but the lamplight.
Your voice scratches and won't retract
even if I hang up and walk free.

But if I keep one ear to myself
it's not to beat you to the last word.
I want the fall that the coin made
before you started to talk like this.

IV
CONTACT

SURVIVORS

If narcissi could talk, they still wouldn't bother.
Contact freezes them. When the wind beheads houses
or the rain's exhaust blackens the spent gardens,

they keep to themselves. They dance indetectably.
Their bulbs are unearthed, their heads still
and fragile from the memory of underground.

They spend days window-shopping in town,
nights tracing bruises on the plaster wall
in the bathroom. They'll walk out with you;

they'll sleep with you, but not kiss you goodbye –
saving that for the dark, a canal bridge
at three in the morning, ice tight on the water;

words form, crystals that hands shake loose:
"Nothing. Don't know. It doesn't feel…"
Oh God, what are you doing out here?

This dizzy spell is an overdose of traffic –
the displaced queens seeing in their own cards
a future of slights and diminishing returns. Each

spring there is less being: the growth stutters,
the bulb is disconnected. It must have
been a dreadful time, to leave them like this.

But when did it happen? They admit nothing
now, held in the shadow of their good looks,
their submission a refusal to be involved.

SANDMAN

You know what the day feels like
after a sleepless night. A coach station
in late spring, rainy with voices,
dissent beaten down by unconcern;
or travelling back from the coast
with sand grains lodged in the folds
of your clothes. The light is cramped.
You never clear the oxygen debt.

Meanwhile, the latent dreams will
have their say in daylight:
a furious proliferation of images,
layer on layer of thin action, compressed;
pages the censor and the pornographer
sat up together to make. Some people
behave as though they never slept;
their memories are only skin deep.

Dreams is too comfortable a word
for the thoughts of mine you hold
in restless hands, a cat's cradle
that you can tighten or unpick.
Does it make you feel strong
to play the sandman with me
like this, to hurt and comfort?
It sounds bitter now, to say:

when I slept with you, the best thing,
and sometimes the only thing, was the sleep.

His eyes blacken with questions.
But the room is dark and still enough
to resolve him, melt the tension
from his shoulders and forehead.

Hard seeds fall through his face
against the window. They knit
together, and forget themselves
in a community. A chemical garden:

pastel colours drawn out in threads,
flowers hardening as the water
flakes off all its involvement.
In a few weeks it is complete:

brilliant, translucent, and single.
An improvised perfection, with no
scope for loss. It only pretends
to grow. For his sake

it had better stay that way.
Time passes. He buys new clothes,
dyes the hair of ageing wives,
sharpens his wit on the telephone.

The sun-ray lamp mends his face,
paints on a new skin. He breathes
a light too fine to see by,
and tells himself he loves everyone.

TIGHTEN

It's best to keep your head down
when the wind blows the sleet back
into the face of sunlight;
or your love pins you to the bed
like a drunk fumbling with a door-key,

and his mouth is a wounded heel.
Don't cough the words; just inhale.
The world carries itself. Labour
is redundant; the red clay titans
are drained, asleep below ground.

Their life has become an outcry.
It pays to keep your mouth shut
when your best friend explains to you
that he let a man beat him senseless
because pain never lets you down.

THE CAPTIVES

My best memory from the sixties
is a glass case in a museum:
BIRDS OF PREY. I was just old enough
to read their names: *owl, falcon,*

eagle, hawk. Their outstretched wings
rippled with light, a still image
that had me falling downstairs
in the attempt to fly. Lost a tooth.

Twenty years later, I felt the glass
shatter in the night. Dust fell
like a gradual rain; the air
pulsed with the beating of wings.

Daylight gave my eyes back lids.
You were watching me. *What's up?*
I reached out and touched you:
the tight skin across your shoulders

stippled with hair, red and gold.
The glass splinters dissolving
into sweat. *I'm here.* A wingtip
brushing the inside of my skull.

SOLVENT

Your kisses dried out his mouth,
made his eyes water. In the park,
under the railway bridge, you gave him
a love that would last. You fucked
his lungs and stole his heart

before he was fifteen. All right,
I'm jealous. You got him first –
left him shivering, wrapped tight
in the nightdress of his own skin,
penetrated by the dawn's arrow

and the bass notes on PCRL's
illicit raggamuffin broadcasts.
Though he dumped you long ago,
no-one can compete with you.
Attention is more real than love:

the slow dissolve. His dark pupils
like cigarette burns in celluloid.
Your attentions drown him. *Keep out
of the reach of children.* He'll chase you
through expensive variants, end up

in debt, in Casualty, in love again.
The streets are paved with ice. It's
in his blue-lipped kiss, bitch.
One night he'll soak himself in you
and burn. Venus. Pure desire.

LAST PHASE OF WINTER

You see him from time to time, never knowing
how he is. Words from him are like snow:
they melt on real skin. His depression
won't kill him, but it will keep him down
for the whole of his life. Each new phase
is just a breaking of ice, a reaching for
the stars embedded in the dark water.

He's so passive, lovers slip through him,
brush flakes of him from their hair.
He builds up theories about "women"
but doesn't learn. Nothing's solid to him,
the cinema has displaced his voice.
He walks behind a screen that's lit
on his side and blank on the world's.

Crowds frighten him: he sees them
as the walking dead. Perhaps that helps.
He has so few ways of framing people.
Death walks in his head all the time;
the sudden makes him panic – most of all
being touched by strangers. In the mirror
he always sees himself turning away.

He has one good answer for everything:
I don't give a fuck. If he slipped
the catch from the razor of his needs,
he'd cut his own eye. He's like a broken
lens, in which all things are reduced
and clear. People use him for that,
to see themselves. He doesn't catch on.

EQUITY

Front legs carries a paper head;
back legs wears a frayed rope.

The midriff is a hollow space
they preserve by moving in time.

After the season, they break it
apart – poor forfeited beast,

with its skeleton of words
held together by a silence.

Sometimes, after the split-up,
one half will stagger around

backstage, trying to close itself
with gestures that mimic wholeness;

while the other, hungry to reform,
holds onto its torn part of hide

and shivers in a bony field, doing
horse – unable to break the habit

or unseat the myth of a rider
whose weight grows on successive nights.

JAYWALKING

Waving his arms in a broken mime,
he dances out into the road
trying to turn every car into a taxi.
Later, he becomes quiet.

There's no comfort in his embrace,
only a tender rage. He folds
himself around you. Soaked
and trembling like a battle-flag,

he fires the gun of his imagination
into himself. He curls up, still;
then leans back against the pillows
and smokes a cigarette.

There's a smudged tattoo on his arm
that, in the half-light, you can't identify;
and this boy is a place you've never
walked through: opposition,

risk, the forest of knotted branches.
He's a stranger in his own life.
You say, *take care*. Like speaking
to a legendary face, or no-one.

VISA

Sitting in the café, you imagine
both sides mistrust you. Who you are
depends on where you're going.
An official fingers your passport.
The photo's out of date, the looks
not holding up so well. Then

they examine your coat for signs
of reversal. And your suitcase,
looking for a false bottom.
You think: *I am not these words*
or any words. Not even this

picture. When they let you pass
you feel as thin as a snapshot,
still damp. If anyone touches you,
your face will stick to their hands.

ENERGY AND SILENCE

Above the vacant offices, a thin wind
tears up a flock of starlings like cinders
in the heat-haze over a bonfire.
In the park, the sun's afterimage
burns its way through a shivering jigsaw

of leaves, peeling from a plaster sky.
The stretching of boughs, loosening of tiles,
draws the wind's shape against the night.
It's dark in these rooms. Behind glass.
The space inside us. Do you know

if all these visions are folded up
into the body? The light is stale there,
written over with creases. You can't reclaim
love from the tissues, the tepid fluids;
they don't carry the banner of freedom.

There's energy in materials. Like
the charge on a door handle; or the face
you can rub into a polythene sheet –
like the Turin Shroud, an artefact
held up as a miracle. Surfaces.

Friction. While birds and electric
cables sing, we huddle in back rooms,
passing on rumours about the body
static: it attracts, it stings. But
it has no power. It does no work.

THE BASSLINE

All day we've been fixed on the bed
like insects shafted by light;
your eyelashes, ribs and pelvis
guarding the hidden shape of fear
as the past talks through us.

You say I should have known
you five years ago. These shadows
press us towards the floor,
the duvet is soaked through.
Furniture is our only security.

It's nearly evening and we're still
not up. Scared of letting go
like a child with a glued model,
you are guilty until proved
innocent. I'm working on it.

FORCEPS

First, grip the head tightly. Try not
to break the skull, which is soft.
Avoid sudden movement; just pull.
The ears offer a good purchase. But

don't risk severing the head. Avoid
twisting, unless the neck is free
and the torso still immersed. Above all
don't clamp the face: you'll crush it.

The use of force requires subtlety.
Stick to the back of the head, or
the temples. Never let go. Be a voice
of reason; apply the correct pressure,

the appropriate torsion. And one day
he'll slip through into maturity.
Give him the forceps. He'll know what
to do: grip, pull, twist, hold on.

JOEL LANE was born in Exeter in 1963 and grew up in Birmingham, where he now lives. His poems and short stories have appeared in a range of magazines and anthologies, including the Stride anthology *Private Cities*. A collection of his short stories, *The Earth Wire*, was published by Egerton Press in 1994; one reviewer commented that "it's a pleasure, albeit a very dark one, to read such elegant and terrifying stories".

He won an Eric Gregory Award for poetry in 1993. *The Edge of the Screen* is his first collection of poems.